MW01493755

KUKRI

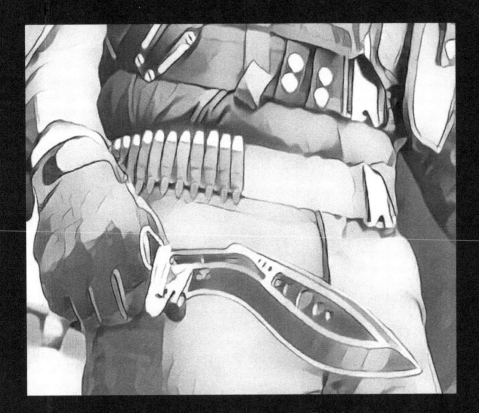

COMBAT KNIFE OF NEPAL
VOLUME ONE

BY

JAMES LORIEGA & FERNAN VARGAS

RAVEN WEAPON SERIES

VOLUME III:

KUKRI

THE COMBAT KNIFE OF NEPAL

A collaborative series between
the Raven Tribe and the Raven Arts Institute

KUKRI

THE COMBAT KNIFE OF NEPAL

JAMES LORIEGA AND FERNAN VARGAS

RAVEN TACTICAL INTERNATIONAL, CHICAGO IL
AND
THE RAVEN ARTS INSTITUTE, NEW YORK, NY

Photo Models:
Mari Cruz Hernandez, Edward Coello, and Stan Brown

DEDICATION

This work is dedicated to the memory of Sensei Ronald Duncan, the **Father of American Ninjutsu**. I met Sensei Duncan in the late 1960s and thus began my long and lasting affinity for all weaponry in general, and for the edge weapon in particular. Although Sensei is best remembered for having brought the Art of Ninjutsu to the public's awareness, his dojo in Brooklyn was home to many combat disciplines, both unarmed and armed.  Training took place six days per week, and when we weren't training in ninjutsu proper or the unarmed Japanese arts, we would work on knife-fighting, knife-throwing, and all manner of exotic weaponry—the Kukri included.

In 1983 we accompanied Sensei to a major martial arts event that was hosted by Temple University in Philadelphia. There, among many other martial arts notables, Sensei introduced us to Dr. Maung Gyi, who first brought the Art of Bando and the use of the Kukri to the US. I would not see Dr. Gyi again until 2004, when he came to New York to conduct invitation-only training with the Kukri.

I have both these men to thank for what little formal aptitude I may possess of the weapon, and if my skill is wanting, then it is only because I have been derelict in applying the great knowledge that was shared with me by these two masters.

4

KUKRI

TABLE OF CONTENTS

AUTHORS' INTRODUCTIONS

The man stood in black attire, starkly contrasted against the once-white canvas of the arena. In his right hand was a Kukri. The blinding lights that surrounded him had no effect on his ability to see, to sense, or to strategize. He called out an unintelligible command and a half-dozen individuals, similarly attired, rose from their seated positions on the canvas floor. Cautiously, they formed a circle around him. In their hands were a variety of Japanese weapons—sticks, chains, short swords, staves, and so on.

Then, the first of the seated individuals ran forward to attack him. His weapon was quickly intercepted and the Kukri in the man's hand flashed out at the attacker's face, describing seven or eight flourishes in the space of three seconds. The attacker fell back, disarmed and negated. Before he hit the canvas floor another attacker was taking his place; but he too met the same fate.

And so it continued with the next three attackers, as their weapons and their attacks were repelled and thwarted. Then came the sixth man; the wary one who had hung back; the one who would need more room to attack without hurting his fellow attackers—with his *katana*.

The sixth man delivered his attacks coldly, skillfully, unemotionally. The man with the Kukri deftly avoided the attacks, vanishing from the katana's trajectory, and causing it to cut … only air. The katana wielder grew impatient. He ran forward to bridge the gap, raised the katana along his right forearm, and delivered a *yoko-giri* horizontal cut intended to slice through everything in its path. As the cut approached him, the man with the Kukri knelt on his right knee, allowing the *katana* to slice the air above his head. Simultaneously, he delivered a series of short horizontal cuts of his own, directed at the katana-wielder's stomach, abdomen, groin, and thighs.

As the man with the katana crumpled, the man with the Kukri rose to face the audience at Madison Square Garden. This had been the final of many demonstrations performed in the allotted thirty minutes. The defeated attackers rose slowly and assembled behind him. As a group, they bowed to the audience three times. As they gathered their vast array of weaponry, the event promoter, Aaron Banks, spoke enthusiastically into the microphone. "Ladies and gentlemen, let's give it up again for Master Ronald Duncan, *the Father of American Ninjutsu*." Applause. Ovation. Exit.

Backstage in our dressing room, a young black belt in our group—who had not previously demonstrated with us—asked, "*Sensei, why did you demonstrate with the Kukri at the end? That's not a traditional ninjutsu weapon.*" A hush fell over the dressing room as the rest of us exchanged glances, not knowing what to expect.

But sensei was not upset, even if this fledgling black belt did not yet understand proper martial arts protocol. He checked his Kukri's polish before packing it in his gear bag and said simply, "*It's not traditional ... but I use the Kukri because it works.*" And then, using one of his oft-heard philosophical pearls, he continued: *"Don't let an adherence to tradition get you killed."*

And that was why we trained with the Kukri.

—James Loriega

New York City 2018

"An hour ago I found him whetting the edge of the great Ghoorka knife which he now always carries with him. It will be a bad lookout for the Count if the edge of that "Kukri" ever touches his throat, driven by that stern, ice-cold hand!"

Bram Stroker
Dracula

Kukris are devastating weapons. The Kukri is so effective that Jonathan Harker used one when preparing to do battle against Count Dracula. Now if the blade is good enough to hunt Dracula, the lord of the Undead, for God's sake think of what it will do to your average guy.

Since the time of Prithvi Narayan Shan, the first king of Nepal, the Nepalese military have been armed with the Kukri. This utilitarian knife has been the trade mark of the Gurkha soldiers. Knife and military culture are abound with fantastic tales of both the Kukri and the Gurkhas who wield them. These tales exist for good reason. Most of them are true. The Gurkha soldiers and their famous Kukris have earned the respect and fear of their enemies on the battle field. The Kukri is especially good for separating the bad guy from his body parts. One good swing has been known to lop off arms, decapitate heads and virtually split a body in two. In the book, **Military Anecdotes**, author Geoffrey Reagan states that, *"Its acclaim was demonstrated in North Africa by one unit's situation report. It reads: "Enemy losses: ten killed, ours nil. Ammunition expenditure nil."*

Like any good student of the blade I began a search for resources and information on the Kukri and its use. I found countless articles on the

Gurkhas, on the design and crafting of Kukri itself but surprisingly few methods of proper instruction. As I continued my investigation I found that there actually is little available on the formal method of instruction of the Kukri used by the Gurkhas.

With my resources exhausted I did what any good knife instructor would do, I began to develop my own material. Along the way I was able to develop what I felt were strong applications of this devastating weapon. It seemed only natural to enlist my frequent co-author and fellow blade instructor Maestro James Loriega to bring you this book.

—Fernan Vargas
Chicago 2018

HISTORY OF THE KUKRI

HISTORY OF THE KUKRI

The **Kukri**, or more correctly *Kukhuri*, is a Nepalese knife with an inwardly curved blade, similar to a machete, which is used as both a tool and as a weapon in Nepal. Traditionally, it considered the basic utility of the Nepalese people. It is a characteristic weapon of the Nepalese Army, the Royal Gurkha Rifles of the British Army, the Assam Rifles, the Assam Regiment, the Garhwal Rifles, the Gurkha regiments of the Indian Army, and of all Gurkha regiment throughout the world, so much so that some English-speakers refer to the weapon as a "Gurkha blade" or "Gurkha knife". The Kukri often appears in Nepalese heraldry and is used in many traditional rituals such as wedding ceremonies.

The history of the blade is often debated. Some believe it comes from western sources such as the Greek Kopis or the Iberian Falcata, while others feel it is native to southeast Asia.

Researchers trace the origins of the blade back to the domestic sickle and the prehistoric bent stick used for hunting and later in hand-to-hand combat. Similar implements have existed in several forms throughout South Asia and were used both as weapons and as tools, such as for sacrificial rituals. Burton (1884) writes that the British Museum housed a large Kukri-like falchion inscribed with writing in Pali. Among the oldest existing Kukri are those belonging to *Drabya*

Shah (circa 1559), housed in the National Museum of Nepal in Kathmandu.

The Kukri came to be known to the Western world when the East India Company came into conflict with the growing Gurkha Kingdom, culminating in the Gurkha War of 1814–1816. The Gurkha regiments in both the British and Indian military are famous for their effectiveness and fighting spirit.

All Gurkha troops are issued with two Kukri, a Service No.1 (ceremonial) and a Service No.2 (exercise); in modern times members of the Brigade of Gurkhas receive training in its use. The weapon gained fame in the Gurkha War and its continued use through both World War I and World War II enhanced its reputation among both Allied troops and enemy forces.

Elsewhere during the Second World War, the Kukri was purchased and used by other British, Commonwealth and US troops training in India, including the Chindits and Merrill's Marauders. The notion of the Gurkha with his Kukri carried on through to the Falklands War.

Today the Kukri continues to be used by the Gurkha regiments and has crossed over to the general knife community where it has found an incredible amount of popularity with blade practitioners and collectors alike.

ANATOMY OF THE KUKRI

ANATOMY OF THE KUKRI

The Kukri knife's physical appearance has not varied significantly throughout its existence. While many experts will quickly list the "proper" dimensions of the knife's component parts, such dimensions matter little in view of the fact that the selection of any weapon is an *individual* matter, subject to personal preference, body type, and fighting style. Essential design elements of the Kukri knife include:

Blade

The Kukri is designed primarily for chopping. The shape varies a great deal from being quite straight to highly curved with angled or smooth spines. There are substantial variations in dimensions and blade thickness depending on intended tasks as well as the region of origin and the smith that produced it. As a general guide the spines vary from 5–10 mm at the handle, and can taper to 2 mm by the point while the blade lengths can vary from 26–38 cm for general use. The two smaller blades are used for sharpening and maintaining the kukri.

A kukri designed for general purpose is commonly 16–18 inches in overall length and weighs approximately 1–2 lbs. Larger examples are impractical for everyday use and are rarely found except in collections or as ceremonial weapons. Smaller ones are of more limited utility, but very easy to carry.

Another factor that affects its weight and balance is the construction of the Kukri. To reduce weight while keeping strength, the blade might be hollow forged, or a *fuller* is created. Kukris are made with several different types of fullers including:

> *tin chira* (triple fuller),
>
> *dui chira* (double fuller),
>
> *angkhola* (single fuller),
>
> or basic non-tapered spines with a large beveled edge.

Notch

Kukri blades usually have a **notch** (alternately called *kaudi*, *kauda*, *karda*, *kaura*, or *cho*) at the base of the blade. Various reasons are given for this, both practical and ceremonial. Among these, that it makes blood and sap drop off the blade rather than running onto the handle; that it delineates the end of the Kukri whilst sharpening; and that it is a symbol representing a cows' foot, or Shiva.

The notch may also represent the teats of a cow, a reminder that the Kukri should not be used to kill a cow, an animal revered and worshipped by Hindus. The notch may also be used as a catch, to hold tight against a belt, or to bite onto twine to be suspended.

Handle

The Kukri handle is most often made of hardwood or water buffalo horn, but ivory, bone, and metal handles have also been produced. The handle quite often has a flared butt that allows better retention in draw cuts and chopping. Most handles have metal bolsters and butt plates which are generally made of brass or steel.

The traditional handle attachment in Nepal is the partial tang, although the more modern versions have the stick tang which has become popular. The full tang is mainly used on some military models, but has not caught-on in Nepal itself.

Scabbard

The Kukri typically comes in either a decorated wooden scabbard or one which is wrapped in leather. Traditionally, the scabbard also holds two smaller blades: an unsharpened **chakmak** to burnish the blade, and another accessory blade called a **karda**. Some older style scabbards also include a pouch for carrying flint or dry tinder.

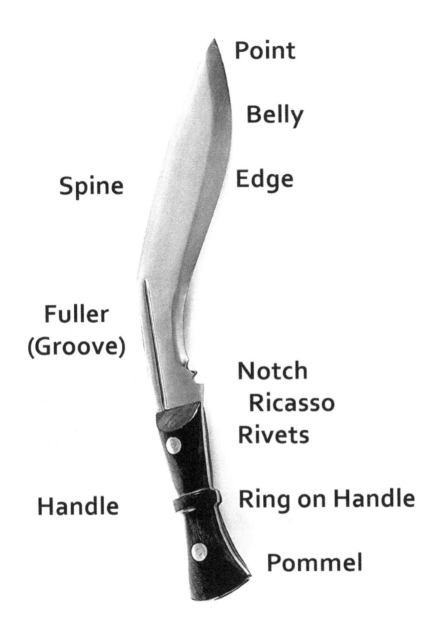

Point

Belly

Edge

Spine

Fuller
(Groove)

Notch
Ricasso
Rivets

Handle

Ring on Handle

Pommel

METHODS OF CARRY

METHODS OF CARRY

There are many ways you can carry the Kukri. It is important to note that the Kukri may not be legal to carry even though it has legitimate and practical reasons why someone may be carrying a Kukri on their person or in their vehicle.

You need to check with the specific laws in your area when it comes to carrying the Kukri. Since many states may consider the Kukri a knife like object and have restrictions as to blade length, you could be in trouble legally if you carry the Kukri.

If you have a Kukri you should also have a sheath for it. A variety of materials are available, from common cloth sheaths, to kydex and leather. Below are examples of carry modes.

The Kukri is normally carried on the hip. This is the most accessible carry. The Kukri can be worn on either side. The Kukri can also be worn in drop leg holsters or even special rigs.

Traditional Gurkha Carry

Milla Jovovich's Dual Carry Rig

COMBAT ATTRIBUTES
OF THE KUKRI

COMBAT ATTRIBUTES OF THE KUKRI

Unlike other knives, the Kukri is a powerhouse. While common knives cut and thrust, the Kukri tears flesh and breaks bone. For this reason, its use is focused more on ripping motions and powerful chopping attacks.

Although the Kukri is not designed for thrusting, its design is well-suited for catching an enemy's blade. Moreover, its curvature makes it difficult for knife-wielding opponents to defend against the Kukri's own attacks. The primary skill is to be able to fend off a bayonet, entrenching tool, club, or similar close quarter weapon.

Those exceptions notwithstanding, a knife—whether simple or specialized—should be relatively easy to employ defensively should your life ever depend on it. In the words of a well known police edged weapons instructor from Massachusetts, speaking of the recent *over-specialization* of knife arts, "It's a **bleep**ing knife: it thrusts; it cuts!"

Now, we are well aware that there can be a knack for properly using certain ethnic knives, but does that mean that the martial artist or blade enthusiast reading this can't effectively defend him/herself with almost any blade they have at hand, formal knife training or otherwise?

The point in all this is that while an official Kukri syllabus of the Gurkha regiments does not exist, its absence in no way impedes your confidence or ability to deploy it in a skilful and efficient manner.

HOW THE KUKRI IS USED

HOW THE KUKRI IS USED

The Kukri has many parallels to another legendary military knife, the *Corvo*. Both are legendary in their respective countries, both are highly effective and feared. Even more significantly, both also lacked a formal methodology for use in combat. Western fencing, *eskrima*, *kenjutsu*, and other arts are often the "parents" to military blade applications. This is not the case with the Kukri; the Kukri, like the *Corvo*, was used in an instinctive manner—by hands that had been conditioned to its use since an early age.

To use the Kukri correctly and effectively, one must first become familiar with its design, weight, balance, and feel. It is best held in a hammer grip, with all four fingers wrapped firmly about the handle and the thumb clamped down on the index. The point faces forward and down toward the opponent's feet. The hand is kept slightly forward of the torso, the forearm and elbow level with the hip.

This book looks at no one historical method of use. What is presented here is a common sense approach based on the strengths and weaknesses of the weapon, and a well rooted understanding of edged weapons. Before entering into the specifics of Kukri use, however, it is important to first understand the laws regarding the use of force in terms of personal protection.

USE OF FORCE

USE OF FORCE

The use of force continuum presented is a general model based on common U.S. use of force guidelines.

Force Continuum

The force continuum is a conceptual tool which exists to aid in determining what level of force is required and justified in controlling the actions of an attacker. *Verbal commands, escort techniques, mechanical controls,* and *deadly force* are all options which are available to a person depending upon the attacker's actions.

Force escalation must cease when the attacker complies with the commands of the individual, and/or the situation is controlled by the individual. The model presented bellow consists of five levels. Physical defensive tactics are appropriate from levels Three to Five.

Level One: The attacker cooperates with your verbal commands. Physical actions are not required.

Level Two: The attacker is unresponsive to verbal commands. Attacker cooperation however is achieved with escort techniques.

Level Three: The attacker actively resists your attempts to control without being assault. Compliance and control holds as well as pain compliance techniques are appropriate actions at this time.

Level Four: The attacker assaults you or another person with actions which are likely to cause bodily harm. Appropriate action would include mechanical controls or defensive tactics such as stunning techniques. Impact and chemical weapons may be appropriate at this level.

Level Five: The attacker assaults you or another person with actions which are likely to cause serious bodily harm or death if not stopped immediately. Appropriate action could include deadly force through mechanical controls, Impact weapons or firearms. Deadly force should be considered only when all avenues for escape have been exhausted, as well as when lesser means have been exhausted, are unavailable or cannot be reasonably employed.

Decision of Force

When making the decision to use force you should use the minimal amount of "reasonable force" necessary to safely control the situation at hand. When using deadly force for self defense you must be prepared to articulate and justify their use of a force.

"Reasonable force" can be defined: *force that is not excessive and is the least amount of force that will permit safe control of the situation while still maintaining a level of safety for himself or herself and the public.*

You may be justified in the use of force when they reasonably believe it to be necessary to defend yourself or another from bodily harm and have no avenue for reasonable escape.

Escalation and de-escalation of resistance and response may occur without going through each successive level. You have the option to escalate or disengage, repeat the technique, or escalate to any level at any time. However, you will need to justify any response to resistance.

Sample Force Continuum

ATTACKER'S ACTION	YOUR RESPONSE
Cooperation	*Verbal Commands*
Passive Resistance	*Escort Control*
Active Resistance	*Control and Compliance Holds*
Assault *which can result in bodily harm*	*Defensive Tactics / Mechanical Controls / Less Lethal Weapons*
Assault *which can result in serious bodily harm or death*	*Deadly Force*

Totality of Circumstances

Totality of circumstances refers to all facts and circumstances known to you at the time. The totality of circumstances includes consideration of the attacker's form of resistance, all reasonably perceived factors that may have an effect on the situation, and the response options available to you.

Sample factors may include the following:

o Severity of the assault or battery

o Attacker is an immediate threat

o Attacker's mental or psychiatric history, if known to you

o Attacker's violent history, if known to you

o Attacker's combative skills

o Attacker's access to weapons

o Innocent bystanders who could be harmed

o Number of attacker's you are facing

o Duration of confrontation

o Attacker's size, age, weight, and physical condition

o Your size, age, weight, physical condition, and defensive tactics expertise

o Environmental factors, such as physical terrain, weather conditions, etc.

In all cases where your assessment and decision are questioned you may need to demonstrate the following:

o That you felt physically threatened by and in danger from the suspect, i.e. that the suspect's behavior (body language / words / actions) were aggressive and threatening;

o   That you used force as a last resort, and that you used the
    reasonable amount;

o   That you stopped using force once you had the suspect and the
    situation under control.

o   That you have exhausted all reasonable efforts to escape the
    situation.

BASIC STANCES

The Combat Stance

The **combat stance** is assumed by standing square with the feet approximately twelve inches apart with the body bladed. The non-dominant leg is planted on the ball of the foot and the knees are slightly bent. The hips and shoulders are in alignment and the torso is kept upright. Do not crouch.

The blade hand is held in front of the body at centerline and the elbow is bent with the tip of the Kukri facing the opponent. It is crucial when adopting this stance that the Practitioner keep their entire body behind the extended blade. No part of the body should be flush with the Kukri or in front of it. The extended blade should be thought of as a shield. If the enemy wishes to attack any part of the Practitioner's anatomy, they must first contend with the Kukri.

The Commando Stance

The **commando stance** presented here is a slight variation of the stance taught throughout WWII by such combative luminaries as William Fairbairn and Rex Applegate. The stance varies from the original taught in WWII in two significant ways:

- *First,* the lead arm is held vertically, not horizontally. Man is a vertical animal. Eyes, throat, heart, etc., basically run down the centerline of the body. The vertical lead arm can help shield these targets better than if it is held horizontal manner.

- *Second*, the knife is held in with a full hand grip, as opposed to a saber grip. The grip is used for maximum weapon retention. A blade held in this fashion is much more difficult to grab or take away. The Kukri itself is a barrier to a grabbing hand by the enemy.

The stance is assumed by blading the body at a 45-degree angle, with the knife held closely to the rear, and the free hand in front, in a vertical position, guarding the body's centerline. This stance is used only against unarmed enemies or as a baiting tactic.

A Practitioner should never assume this stance when facing another similarly-armed enemy. There are several reasons for this:

First, an unarmed enemy is likely to focus on immobilizing the Practitioner's Kukri. By keeping the Kukri to the rear, the free hand is able to act as an obstacle to this goal by striking, parrying, and redirecting the enemy.

Second, while the free hand can be very useful against an unarmed foe, it is an easy target for the enemy's weapon.

When the Practitioner blades their body and keeps the free hand in front as a vertical shield, he is properly prepared to contend with an empty hand assailant. The bladed body structure and free hand to the front provide good bio-mechanical structure for addressing incoming blows. Against an edged weapon attack, however, this structure would be more or a liability than an advantage.

BASIC GRIPS

The Forward Grip

The Forward grip is executed by taking the knife in the hand in a firm yet relaxed manner. The hand will form a fist around the knife handle with the thumb resting on the index finger. The edge of the Kukri should be facing away from the Practitioner and in alignment with the Practitioner's middle knuckle line tip up to the sky.

Many instructors will advocate a modified version of this grip, often called a saber grip. In the saber grip the Practitioner's thumb will rest on the spine of the Kukri. While this gives additional support through strong skeletal alignment, I do not recommend this grip. The reason being that a strong "blade beat", or even inadvertent jamming can easily dislodge the weapon. If this grip is used it should be done so sparingly once the Practitioner is in the midst of an attack. It should also be noted that the stripping defense methods found in south East Asian martial arts are often less effective against the Forward grip. The Forward grip should be used when maximum range is desired as t allows the Practitioner to more effectively work from the long range.

The Reverse Grip

The Reverse grip is executed by taking the knife in the hand in a firm yet relaxed manner. The hand will form a fist around the knife handle with the thumb resting on the index finger. The edge of the blade should be facing away from the Practitioner and in alignment with the Practitioner's middle knuckle line tip down to the ground. When gripping knives with no substantial guard, the Practitioner should place their thumb on the top of the handle.

St. Andrew's Grip

St. Andrew's grip is executed by taking the knife in the hand in a firm yet relaxed manner. The hand will form a fist around the knife handle with the thumb resting on the index finger. The free hand will bring the knife hand at the wrist. The knife hand can be in either Forward or Reverse orientation. The edge of the blade can either face toward or away from the Practitioner. Due to the additional pressure exerted by the supporting hand, this grip can be used for extremely deep penetration on cuts and thrusts.

FOOTWORK

FOOTWORK

For the Practitioner, good
footwork is paramount. There is
arguably no aspect of the fighting
arts more important than
footwork. The Practitioner will
be well served to develop through
drill and practice, flowing and
quick footwork. Precision
however, is more important than
speed. The footwork of the

Practitioner must be precise in both offensive and defensive actions in
order to ensure success. A Practitioner can use good footwork to help
control the scenario and maintain an advantage. Lack of proper
footwork will make victory nearly impossible for the Practitioner.
Proper footwork however can help to offset other weaknesses in a
Practitioner's repertoire.

In any encounter a Practitioner can use linear movement both forward
and backward, diagonal movement (45-degrees) forward or backward,
and horizontal movement from side to side. It is crucial that the
Practitioner learn to move smoothly in every direction, both on the
advance and the retreat.

Whenever the Practitioner initiates an attack they should initially seek to identify the angle which will offer least resistance to their attack. By capitalizing on the least defended angle the Practitioner improves their odds of successfully completing their attack. This means that the Practitioner should attack on an open line, or attack after proactively opening an enemy's line. When on the defensive, the Practitioner should seek to identify the angle which is absent of aggressive force, in doing so the Practitioner rather than clashing with the enemy will simply evade or escape.

The Advance

To **advance**, refers to any time the Practitioner takes steps towards the Enemy. The goal of any Practitioner is to always attempt to establish proper distance from the enemy which places the Practitioner in a position of advantage. There are times in which advancing steps are necessary to accomplish this. A Practitioner may therefore advance to gain the proper range to complete an attack or to jam or pass an enemy

The Retire

To **retire** refers to any time the Practitioner takes steps away from the Enemy. The goal of any Practitioner is to always attempt to establish proper distance from the enemy which places the Practitioner in a position of advantage. There are times in which retreating steps are necessary to accomplish this. A Practitioner may therefore retire after making a successful attack in order to be at a safer distance.

Warrior Walking

Warrior walking is just what the name implies. It is walking, a natural foot over foot way of walking. Like most people in the martial arts I was first taught how to "properly" move, step and slide, step and shuffle etc. It was not until I met Mescalero Apache knife instructor, Mr. Fred Teather, that I learned the value of just naturally walking. In his family system of knife work, Lopez advocates natural walking because it is faster, more fluid and more natural than a shuffle step.

At first analysis I thought it was a flawed idea. Upon applying natural walking in practice and sparring my teachers lesson was confirmed. The natural step allowed me to move with greater fluidity. In most martial arts the student relies on proper stance for defense and power generation. In order to be ready the student must maintain this stance even while in movement. To this end the martial artist must move in a certain way as to preserve their structure. In knife combat, the blade does a considerable amount of the work for the artist. The artist is therefore not tied to a particular structure in order to generate power. Because of this consideration, the natural walking is permissible.

Forward 45-Degree Step

The Practitioner will use a triangular footwork pattern to move toward the subject and inside the weapon's arc of danger. The Practitioner begins by standing with the feet together on the tip of an imaginary triangle or the bottom of an imaginary "V".

Moving to the Right

While picturing an assailant standing in front of the Practitioner he or she will take a moderate step forward on a 45-degree angle to the right with the right foot. The back or left foot will remain stationary or will shuffle forward slightly.

Moving to the Left

While picturing an assailant standing in front of the Practitioner he or she will take a moderate step forward on a 45-degree angle to the left with the left foot. The back or right foot will remain stationary or will shuffle forward slightly. This simple stepping pattern allows us to move off-line of the attack, inside the arc of danger while still allowing us to move into the assailant for follow-up control.

Reverse 45-Degree Step

The reverse triangle is the reverse of the female triangle. In this pattern the Practitioner will move backwards on a 45- degree angle.

Moving to the Right

While picturing an assailant standing in front of the Practitioner he or she will take a moderate step backwards on a 45-degree angle to the right with the right foot. The back or left foot will remain stationary or will shuffle forward slightly.

Moving to the Left

While picturing an assailant standing in front of the Practitioner he or she will take a moderate step backwards on a 45-degree angle to the left with the left foot. The back or right foot will remain stationary or will shuffle forward slightly.

Forward Pivot

The **forward pivot** is performed by turning on the ball of your lead foot while simultaneously swinging your rear leg forward in front of you.

Rear Pivot

The **rear pivot** is executed by turning on the ball of the rear foot while simultaneously swinging your lead leg to the back.

Lateral Evasion

The **lateral evasion** is performed by stepping quickly to the right or the left. If stepping right, step your right foot out first then bring your left over and assume a well balanced posture. When stepping left, step your left foot out first and then bring your right over and assume a well balanced posture.

DEFENSIVE TECHNIQUES

DEFENSIVE TECHNIQUES

I was an on duty EMT responding to a call. Everything seemed like a medical call when we came through the door but moments into our evaluation things went south. As I attempted to reach down for my blood pressure cuff the young man jumped up and grabbed a full sized kitchen knife off the cluttered counter and swiped at my face. I jerked my head back, as the blade passed by my face, then I hollowed out at the core when the blade swept back across the path that would have been my gut.

—Jesse Lawn
Ninjutsu Instructor

This story was recounted to me during my research by Jesse Lawn. Mr. Lawn successfully used the defensive concept of voiding the body to protect himself against an emotionally disturbed patient who made serious efforts to kill him. Mr. Lawn's account clearly illustrates the "Sway" and "Deer" techniques. Both techniques are based on instinctive body reaction; this is one of the reasons why they are so effective. They fine-tuned variations of a movement that the body wishes to do instinctively when in danger.

In the world of fighters there is an old adage, "The best defense is not being there."

We hold this adage to be true and it is a corner stone of our defensive maneuvers and philosophy. While checking hands and blocking techniques are a necessary part of any Practitioner's repertoire, I

58

would like to pay special attention to the art of voiding the body as a means of defense.

In this chapter we will be looking at the defensive concept of *Voiding the Body*. In the **Way of the Raven System,** Voiding the Body takes a more prevalent role in defense than blocking or checking.

Voiding the body is simply explained as follows:
When the enemy attacks any part of the Practitioner's anatomy, the Practitioner will remove said target from area of attack, thus protecting it from harm. This is done in a number of ways. In his writings, fencing master Ridolfo Capo Ferro suggested that a good swordsman will always follow up a parry or a voiding of the body with a counter-attack.

To Void or to Check, That is the Question ...

The majority of the knife work we see in other schools and through video media is extremely reliant on the use of the checking hand. For example, there are various drills that are popular training tools and make their practitioners very good at checking. The level of hand speed and coordination is greatly enhanced by these drills and, at first glance, they seem to be an effective way of training. However, it is not until one begins training in the European and Western arts that one truly realizes the value of footwork and body voids as a means of effective defense.

One of my instructors, Guru Brandt Smith once told me not to be *lazy*. He explained to me that footwork and body voids are essential to defense. It wasn't until after I was able to properly use footwork and body voids that Guru Brandt introduced the checking hands. I had a similar experience with Mr. Fred Teather. Blocking was not frowned upon, but if you could defend with movement, you were expected to.

Interestingly this concept is not limited to blade work. The famous bare-knuckle boxer Mendoza also advocated voiding the body over using parries. I reflect back on Guro Brandt telling me not to be lazy. Laziness? Yes, he was right. I see it all the time. You can get away with using improper or underdeveloped footwork without too many negative consequences if you're able to use the checking hand to compensate. Therein lies the real problem.

I personally feel much more comfortable using movement to defend myself. In spite of my personal preference, I realize there is a need to train both aspects of defense. I therefore go on the record with this statement: If you are using the checking hand to compensate for poor footwork/body movement, you are training incorrectly. You should instead should be using your checking hands to complement your footwork/body movement. This requires that you develop *both* skills to a functional level and use them at the appropriate time, and under the appropriate circumstances.

If I am fighting in an open parking lot, I should then be using movement as my primary defense. If I take a good cut to the checking hand to the point that it is disabled, using it may be a moot point. I will have no choice but to use footwork. Similarly, I may defending in a narrow corridor, or between parked cars? Or I may have taken a disabling cut to the leg(s)? In such situations footwork may not be an option so I sure as hell better know how to use that checking hand.

The Sway

When an attack comes at a high line, the Practitioner simply throws their shoulders backwards taking the head outside the arc of danger. The Practitioner will pull their chin to their chest and bring their hands under their chin while shrugging the shoulders. This combination of movement offers the Practitioner the greatest amount of protection. By tucking the chin and shrugging the shoulders the Practitioner is "shielding the carotid arteries. Bringing in the hands close under the chin keeps the hands from remaining out in the open where they can easily be cut.

The Hollow

When an attack comes at a low line, the Practitioner will hollow out their abdomen and throw their hips and buttocks backwards taking the torso outside the arc of danger. The Practitioner's back will curl like a letter "C" allowing the hands will to come forward as a counter balance, and possible attack. In both cases the hands come up as a counter balance and more importantly to protect the vital areas.

Reassemblement

Reassemblement is the action of withdrawing the lead leg to the rear either to or past the rear leg. The reassemblement is used as a defensive technique as it voids the leg from possible attack. The final posture of the movement closely resembles the defensive **deer** technique described above.

The Duck

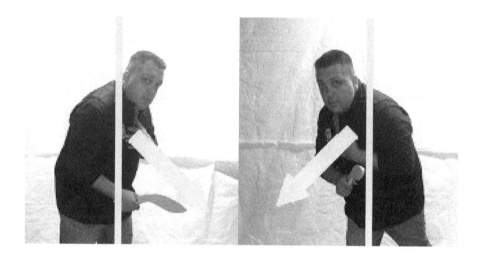

There are times when the best defense for a Practitioner is to drop their level in order to avoid an attack to the high line. To execute a **duck** the Practitioner must lower their level. This is achieved not by bending at the waist or lowering the head by bending the neck but by bending the legs while keeping the back and neck straight. This is done so that the Practitioner can keep their eyes on the enemy at all times.

The Slip

The **slip** is an evasive movement of the head used to avoid incoming linear attacks. Just as in boxing, the Practitioner will move their head and shoulders off line as to evade the attack. One trick taught to me by my old boxing coach was to imagine throwing your shoulder at the incoming attack. This naturally creates the body mechanics needed to execute the movement correctly

Blade Blocking

It is advisable that a Practitioner block with their blade rather than cut through an attack. Practitioner's should push their blade out towards an attack and absorb the attack on their blade. The reason for using this method rather than cutting into an attack is that even if a Practitioner successfully cuts the attacking limb, the cut may be ineffective for several reasons. Those reasons could include:

- a knife can not cut through heavy clothing

- knife cuts attacks athe limb but cut fails to stop momentum of the attack

- a Practitioner may be using an improvised weapon which lacks a sharpened edge

When working with smaller blades, the blocks will be made against the enemy's flesh. When working with larger blades the Practitioner may have the option to block blade on blade. If the Practitioner is to block blade on blade they should avoid blocking edge to edge. Blocking flat to edge or even spine to edge is a much more effective way of blocking as it is less likely to damage the important cutting edge of the Practitioner's knife.

Lines of Defense

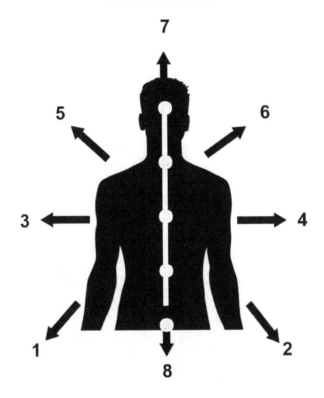

Blocking techniques will be executed on particular lines of interception. A direct thrust can come at any elevation on the vertical line. In addition to this attack virtually all other attacks will come along one of the points on 8 line, illustrated above. The most common angles of defense used are on the horizontal line are angles 3 and 4; on the vertical line, angles 7 and 8. A Practitioner can make slight adjustments to adequately defend the diagonal lines in between. For this reason most illustrations and photos of defensive techniques in this book reflect the four fundamental lines of interception with the clear understanding that there are eight lines in total, four *primary* and four *secondary*.

High Block

A **high block** is executed against a vertical attack coming from high to low. Forcefully thrust your arms up at approximately a 45-degree angle from your body. The elbows are bent but there is enough muscular tension in the arms to absorb the impact and deter the attack.

Low Block

The **low block** is executed against a vertical attack coming from low to high. Forcefully thrust your arms down at approximately a 45-degree angle from your body. The elbows are bent but there is enough muscular tension in the arms to absorb the impact and deter the attack.

Outside Block

The **outside block** is executed against a linear or circular attack coming toward the Practitioner. Forcefully thrust the forearm outwards towards the attack from the inside of the body to the outside of the body. The Practitioners hand should not cross much farther than the shoulder. The arm is held at a 45-degree angle. The elbows are bent but there is enough muscular tension in the arms to absorb the impact and deter the attack.

Inside Block

The **inside block** is executed against a linear or circular attack coming toward the Practitioner. Forcefully sweep the arm in front of the body from outside of the body to the inside of the body across the centerline. Note that the Practitioners hand should not cross farther than the shoulder. The arm is held at a 45-degree angle. The elbows are bent but there is enough muscular tension in the arms to absorb the impact and deter the attack.

Roof Block

There are two **roof blocks** that are used to cover the *right* and the *left* side of the body and protecting the head and neck. They are so named because the forearm and the blade form a frame similar to the roof of a house. The blade is held at a right angle to the forearm, and the gripping hand is raised above the head. The Kukri's edge faces in the blocking direction. The roof block is best used with a larger weapon such as a bowie knife or a machete.

To execute the **inside roof block** the Practitioner will raise his weapon hand as if executing an empty hand upward block. The Practitioner's head will be in between their arm and their weapon which will be pointing tip down. The strike of the enemy will land on the Practitioner's weapon. The Practitioner should step on a 45-

degree angle away from their weapon so that the enemy's strike glances instead of hitting with full force.

To execute the **outside roof block** (often called a ***wing block***) the Practitioner will raise his elbow so that their weapon hand goes to the rear and the weapons tip points downward. Some choose to rest the weapon onto the arm/shoulder closest to it. The Practitioner's arm and weapon should form the shape of an "A" on the outside of the Practitioner's body. The strike of the enemy will land on the Practitioner's weapon. The Practitioner should step on a 45-degree angle away from their weapon so that the enemy's strike glances instead of hitting with full force.

Sweeping Block

To execute the **sweeping block** the Practitioner will drop the point of their weapon towards the floor from the outside of their body and then sweep across to the inside. This defense is used primarily against a foreword thrust to the midsection.

Reverse Grip Outside Parry

Reverse Grip Inside Parry

Live Hand Parry

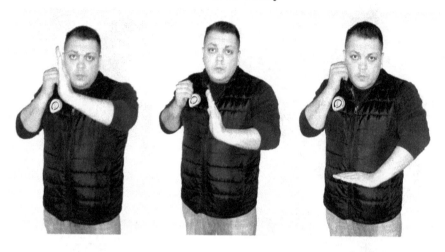

The **live hand** is used to parry or redirect attacks. In order to use the live hand for defense the Practitioner will use an open hand to slap, or push the oncoming attack of the enemy. A parrying motion should be short and crisp. A Practitioner should not over extend their body when executing the parry. The goal of the parry is not to be an obstacle to the enemy's attack but rather to deviate its trajectory away from its target by altering its course. The parry can be used effectively pushing an attack to the inside, to the outside, and downward.

CONFLICT ANATOMY
AND PHYSIOLOGY

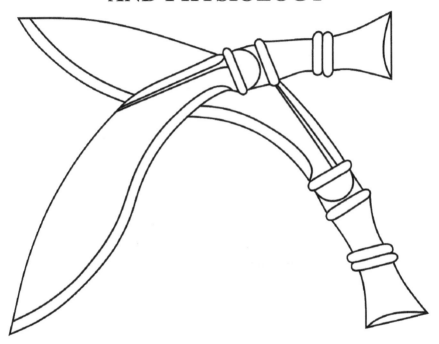

CONFLICT ANATOMY

Targeting

You should always keep in mind that the Kukri is a deadly weapon and can cut through muscle and bone. It can also kill. Using the Kukri is using deadly force and unless you feel your life or the life of another is in danger of GREAT BODILY HARM OR DEATH, you should not use the Kukri. You may have to explain your actions in court. Some of the situations that the court may consider your actions justified include these factors:

(1) Did the individual attacking you have a weapon and what kind of weapon did he have?

(2) Did the attacker have the means and ability to cause you great bodily harm or death.

(3) Were there multiple attackers. (4) Was there no way to escape from your attacker?

(5) Was there a way to call the police?

(6) Who started the fight?

(7) Was there no other way to avoid a physical conflict?

(8) Was there a way to handle the subject without using deadly force?

(9) Did you really feel your life was in danger?

10) Why were you carrying a Kukri?

Considering that using the Kukri is considered deadly force the following target areas should be considered if you have to protect your life or the life of another person.

Types of Edged Weapon Targets

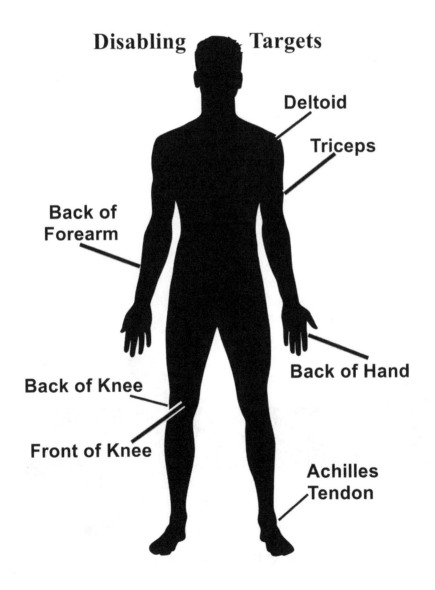

Disabling Targets

Deltoid

Triceps

Back of Forearm

Back of Hand

Back of Knee

Front of Knee

Achilles Tendon

Disabling attacks are those brought to targets that when cut or damaged are most certain to stop or seriously impair mobility or function. Like any wound a disabling attack can be lethal, but is rarely so if medical attention can be acquired in a reasonable amount of time.

Targets include:

    (1) Back of the hand,

    (2) Back of the forearm,

    (3) Deltoid,

    (4) Triceps,

    (5) Front of the Knee,

    (6) Back of the knee/hamstring,

       (7) Achilles tendon

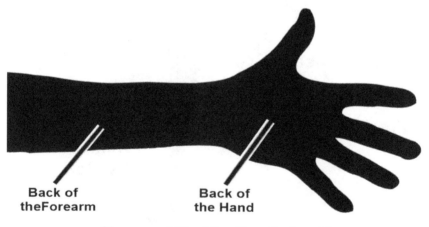

Back of theForearm   **Back of the Hand**

Close-up of Disabling Targets 1 and 2

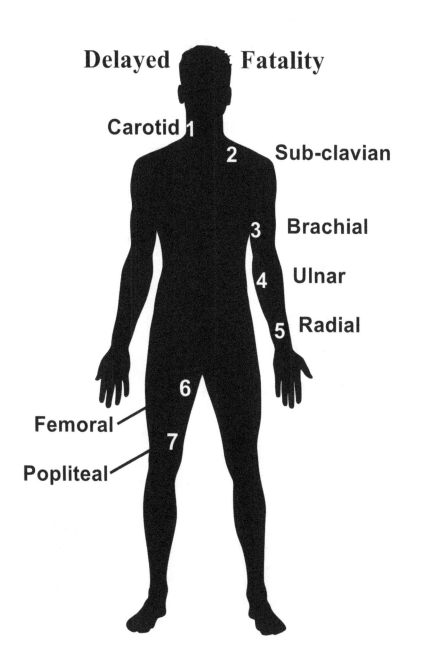

Delayed   Fatality

Carotid 1

2 Sub-clavian

3 Brachial

4 Ulnar

5 Radial

6

Femoral

7

Popliteal

There are targets on the human body which when cut or damaged will result in a more or less certain fatality if not treated immediately. Without proper medical the injured individual will die due to blood loss. The injured party will likely experience light headedness, unconsciousness, and eventually die from blood loss. The rate at which impairment occurs can vary from relatively quick to relatively slow. This means that a Practitioner must be aware that even if they have received this type of wound they still have a viable chance of fighting through and controlling the situation. The survival mindset at this point is imperative for the Practitioner.

Targets include:

    (1) Carotid artery

    (2) Sub-clavian artery

    (3) Brachial artery

    (4) Ulnar artery

    (5) Radial artery

    (6) Femoral artery

    (7) Popliteal artery.

FAST KILLS

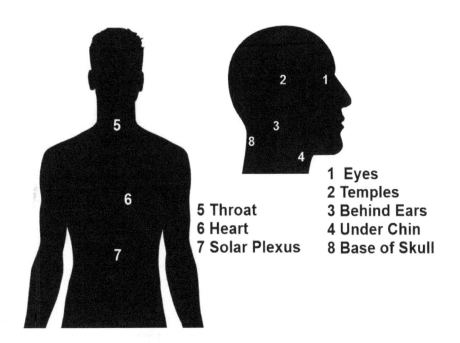

1 Eyes
2 Temples
3 Behind Ears
4 Under Chin
8 Base of Skull

5 Throat
6 Heart
7 Solar Plexus

Fast kill targets when cut or damaged will be almost immediately fatal. It is paramount that the Practitioner protect these targets areas at all times and at all costs. The sacrificing of another non-vital body part in the protection of these targets is obviously acceptable and should be employed if needed. For example, if a subject stabs at a Practitioner's eye, and the Practitioner has no option for movement, it would be acceptable for the Practitioner to cover their eye sacrificing the hand in order to avoid a fatal wound.

Targets include:

    (1) Brain via eye socket

    (2) Brain via temple

    (3) Brain via space behind the ear

    (4) Brain via space under the chin

    (5) Throat

    (6) Heart

    (7) Solar Plexus

    (8) Base of the Skull.

It is crucial that Practitioners learn the edged weapon targets for two reasons:

(1) The Practitioner can better protect themselves if they know which parts of their body are the most crucial to protect.

(2) The Practitioner can better decide appropriately as to what level of force to use since they will have a clear understanding of what their application to each body target will accomplish. Practitioner must know what targets are most likely to stop the action of the assault.

OFFENSIVE FUNDAMENTALS

OFFENSIVE FUNDAMENTALS

The Kukri's relatively simple (though wicked) design allows it to be used in a somewhat intuitive and very effective manner. The casual reader interested in personal protection needs merely to hold the Kukri firmly as if it were a sickle (which it strongly resembles) and slash in the direction of the threat. For the reader or the edged weapons enthusiast who wants to exploit every possible application of the knife, there follow the quasi-official instructions on the knife's use as they are taught and disseminated by those trained to be the most adept in its use—the Gurkhas.

Military training being what it is in most countries, the fighting movements taught by the Gurkhas follow the universal KISS principle. Their core, with very little exception, is the same as was devised by Achille Marrozzo in the 15th century Italy, in Japan during the Feudal era, and in the Philippines long before the Spaniards set foot on the islands.

The Kukri, however, is not a conventional weapon and to use it correctly and effectively, the wielder must first become familiar with its design, weight, balance, and feel.

Angles of Attack

Striking techniques, thrusts or swings will be executed on particular lines of attack. All other attacks will come on one of the lines illustrated below. There are 11 angles of attack, of which 8 are the primary work horse angles used for common defense. For this reason the majority of the striking techniques shown in this book are only used demonstrating the essential 8 angles. The reader however should know that there are an additional 3 angles that can be used.

Eight Essential Cut and Thrust Angles

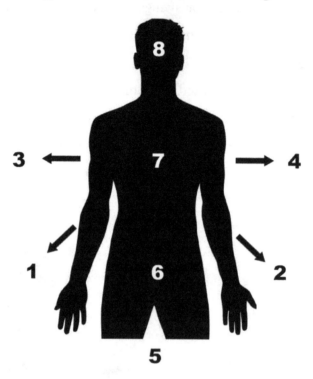

Angle 1:   Forehand downward diagonal

Angle 2:   Backhand downward diagonal

Angle 3:   A horizontal swing to the Inside

Angle 4:   A horizontal swing to the out side

Angle 5:   Forehand Upward diagonal

Angle 6-8: A jabbing, lunging, or punching attack directed straight toward the Practitioner's front. It can be delivered from any height.

Full Eleven Cut and Thrust Aangles

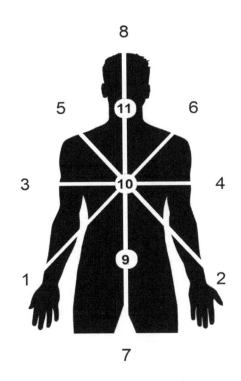

Angle 1:   Forehand downward diagonal

Angle 2:   Backhand downward diagonal

Angle 3:   A horizontal swing to the Inside

Angle 4:   A horizontal swing to the out side

Angle 5:   Forehand Upward diagonal

Angle 6:   Backhand Upward diagonal

Angle 7:   Upward vertical

Angel 8   Downward Diagonal

Angle 9-11:   A jabbing, lunging, or punching attack directed straight
toward the Practitioner's front. It can be delivered from any height.

THRUSTING TECHNIQUES

THRUSTING TECHNIQUES

The thrust can be performed in two ways. The first is by simply extending the arm. The second is performed by extending the arm and expanding the body. This expansion is achieved by extending the blade arm forward while simultaneously pulling the live hand to the rear of the body. This motion will expand the Practitioner's chest. The motion is similar to drawing a bow and arrow.

The Four Cardinal Directions of the Thrust

There are four categories of thrust based on the area from which the attack originates and hand position.

1. The **vertical descending** thrust
2. The **inside thrust** (coming from the outside of the body toward the inside)
3. The **outside thrust** (coming from the inside of the body toward the outside)
4. The **vertical ascending** thrust

In addition to categorization based on point of origin, the thrust can be categorized by level of depth achieved in the execution of the attack. Shallow thrusts entering *less* than two inches are referred to as **piercing attacks**. Thrusts penetrating *more* than two inches into the target are referred to as **stabbing attacks**.

In order to facilitate removal of the knife, and to create a larger wound channel, the Practitioner should turn his knife after a successful thrust in a "U" or comma shape before attempting to pull the knife back out.

The Angle of the Thrust

Fencing master Puck Curtis in his article, **Spanish Fencing notation Part 3:** *Fighting Distance*, explains that in his work Spanish fencing master Carranza identifies the *Right Angle* as providing one the best reach. If the hand is elevated, the angle becomes *obtuse*. If the hand is lowered the angle becomes *acute*. Both the obtuse and acute angles have *less* reach than the Right Angle.

The Lunge

To perform a **lunge attack** the Practitioner will extend the knife arm until it is slightly higher than the shoulder. The lead leg will bend bringing the knee forward. Ideally the Practitioner should have their front knee just above the instep of the leading foot. The rear leg will be at full extension with the rear foot flat on the floor. In this attack the free hand can be swung to the rear for counter balance.

Standing Lunge

The **standing lunge** differs slightly from the traditional lunge. To execute the standing lunge the Practitioner must extend the blade arm and then shift their weight forward over the dominant leg while straightening the real leg. The movement is not as committed or dramatic as the traditional lunge. The Practitioner will find that their foot placement is not nearly as wide as in a standard lunge. In this attack the free hand can be swung to the rear for counter balance or the live hand be kept close to the chest.

Rear Leg Lunge or Reverse Lunge

The **rear leg lunge** is virtually identical to a standard lunge with two exceptions. To execute the rear leg lunge the Practitioner will begin from guard position. The Practitioner will bring their lead leg back while extending their blade arm to attack. The Practitioner is in effect lunging on their non-dominant side. The Practitioner may also keep the live hand forward rather than backwards as in a traditional lunge.

CUTTING TECHNIQUES

CUTTING TECHNIQUES

The cut is an attack that uses the edge of the weapon. In combat cuts can be shallow or profound. All cuts are made with a circular pattern as opposed to a straight line. The nature of circular momentum vs. linear momentum allows for faster flow from one attack to the next. Cutting in a circle rather than a straight line also helps the Kukri to naturally return to the point of origin. When executing a cut the attack should begin from the chosen guard and extend outwards for the cut and then return to the chosen guard with the point of the Kukri oriented towards the enemy. The smaller you make the circle, the faster you will make the cut. The larger the circle the more powerful the cut will be. For our purposes the cut can be divided into three categories regardless of the angle or target at which they are applied.

The Slashing Cut

The **slashing cut** is delivered in a rapid manner. It accelerates towards the target, makes contact and is retracted all in one fluid motion.

The Draw Cut

The **draw cut** is delivered in a rapid manner. It accelerates towards the target, makes contact and then lingers for a split second. Once the Kukri has been placed on its target the Practitioner will then retract the blade with increased pressure drawing it back to guard. This cut occurs in two distinct motions. First placing the Kukri and second, drawing it back. This type of cut is not as fast as the slashing cut but offers increased penetration.

The Pressure Cut

The **pressure cut** is the slowest of the three types of cuts but what it sacrifices in speed it makes up for in sheer power. A properly executed pressure cut can utterly destroy its target. The pressure draw cut is delivered with the same mechanics as a slashing cut or draw cut with one additional modification. In a pressure cut the Practitioner will use the free hand to reinforce the hand holding the blade. Together both hands will apply as much pressure as possible during the cut. This increased pressure guarantees an incredibly deep and penetrating wound.

Print depicting the use of kukris during the Lushai Expedition

Five Basic Cuts from the Forward Grip

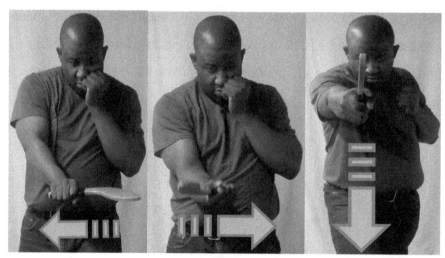

Forward Grip: **Diagonal Forehand Cut**

To execute the forehand diagonal cut, the Practitioner raises the Kukri to shoulder level and then swings downward on the diagonal line.

Forward Grip: **Diagonal Backhand Cut**

To execute the back hand diagonal cut, the Practitioner raises the Kukri to shoulder level and then swings downward on the diagonal line.

Forward Grip: **Horizontal Forehand Cut**

To execute the forehand horizontal cut, the Practitioner holds the Kukri to their side and then swings horizontally across the body.

Forward Grip: **Horizontal Backhand Cut**

To execute the backhand horizontal cut, the Practitioner holds the Kukri to their inside and then swings horizontally across the body.

Forward Grip: **Downward Vertical Cut**

To execute the vertical cut, the Practitioner raises Kukri to shoulder level and then swings downward on the vertical line.

Five Basic Cuts from the Reverse Grip

Reverse Grip: **Diagonal Forehand Cut**

To execute the forehand diagonal cut, the Practitioner raises the Kukri to shoulder level and then swings downward on the diagonal line.

Reverse Grip: **Diagonal Backhand Cut**

To execute the back hand diagonal cut, the Practitioner raises the Kukri to shoulder level and then swings downward on the diagonal line.

Reverse Grip: **Horizontal Forehand Cut**

To execute the forehand horizontal cut, the Practitioner holds the Kukri to their side and then swings horizontally across the body.

Reverse Grip: **Horizontal Backhand Cut**

To execute the backhand horizontal cut, the Practitioner holds the Kukri to their inside and then swings horizontally across the body.

Reverse Grip: **Downward Vertical Cut**

To execute the vertical cut, the Practitioner raises the Kukri to shoulder level and then swings downward on the vertical line.

Five Basic Cuts from St. Andrew's Grip

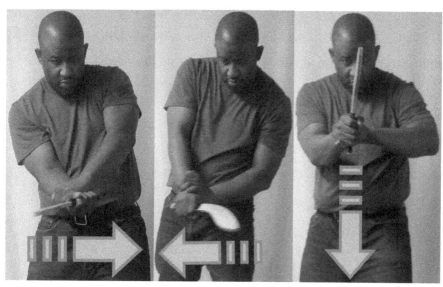

St. Andrew's Grip: **Diagonal Forehand Cut**

To execute the forehand diagonal cut, the Practitioner raises the Kukri to shoulder level and then swings downward on the diagonal line.

St. Andrew's Grip: **Diagonal Backhand Cut**

To execute the back hand diagonal cut, the Practitioner raises the Kukri to shoulder level and then swings downward on the diagonal line.

St. Andrew's Grip: **Horizontal Forehand Cut**

To execute the forehand horizontal cut, the Practitioner holds the Kukri to their side and then swings horizontally across the body.

St. Andrew's Grip: **Horizontal Backhand Cut**

To execute the backhand horizontal cut, the Practitioner holds the Kukri to their inside and then swings horizontally across the body.

St. Andrew's Grip: **Downward Vertical Cut**

To execute the vertical cut, the Practitioner will raises Kukri to shoulder level and then swings downward on the vertical line.

Downward Wind

The **downward wind** is a cutting motion made by rotating the Kukri clockwise into a downward cut. The rotation is made from the elbow, not the shoulder. The downward wind is usually executed in twos. Like the "Steel Wheel," the downward wind can be used in rapid succession for defense. The extended blade should be thought of as a shield. If the enemy wishes to reach any part of the Practitioner's body they must first contend with the Kukri.

Upward Wind

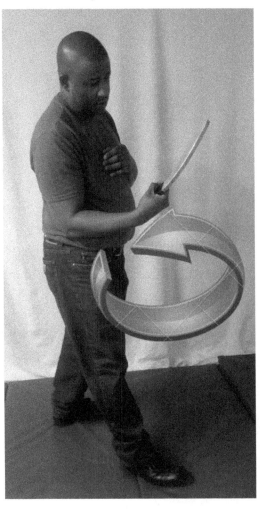

The **upward wind** is a cutting motion made by rotating the Kukri counter clockwise into an upward cut. The rotation is made from the elbow, not the shoulder. The upward wind is usually executed in twos. Like the "Steel Wheel" the upward wind can be used in rapid succession for defense. The extended blade should be thought of as a shield. If the enemy wishes to reach any part of the Practitioner's body they must first contend with the Kukri.

Back Cut

The **back cut** is a circular motion which utilized the false edge of the Kukri. The Practitioner can utilize the back cut from the outside of the body to the inside or from the inside of the body to the outside. The motion from either side is a swooping circular motion using the false edge or spine of the blade as the point of impact. The inside to outside back cut is also extremely effective as a parrying motion.

Axing

Axing is a fully committed power cut. The Practitioner will begin by stepping through with the strong side leg and simultaneously drop the Kukri from the high position down into their target. As the Kukri makes contact, the Practitioner will sink into a deep sitting stance, allowing their entire body weight to pull through in the attack. At the end of the attack the Practitioner will allow their attacking forearm to make contact with their thigh. This contact will prevent injury by preventing the Practitioner from cutting into their own leg.

Snapping Turtle/Snap Cut

The **snapping turtle** attack is flexible and fluid attack that is executed with a whipping motion. The Practitioner will extend the blade hand out to the target and then retract it rapidly, in the same fashion that they would crack a whip.

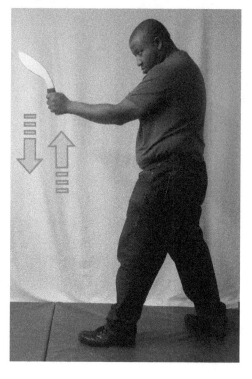

The attack can be made vertically, horizontal or diagonally. The Practitioner can use the spine of the Kukri, the flat of the blade or the edge. This attack is often criticized as not being a true cut. This is an accurate statement. It is not a true cut bound by proper cutting dynamics. The reader need only imagine the amount of damage created by whipping a quarter pound of steel into an adversary. It is neither a cut or a thrust but a devastating maneuver nonetheless.

The Styers Cut

CQC Legend John Styers taught the "vertical cut" in a manner that was very much unique to him and his writing. We will refer to this cut as *the Styers cut* and reprint the instructions in his own words from his classic book on Close Quarter Combat, **Cold Steel**.

The thrust is the foundation of the cut. With the thrust you take your knife to the target. If a full thrust does not strike the target the natural whipping action will take place. This whip is the cut. The Vertical Cut is a thrust which ends abruptly with the thumb up, the nails to the left. When this thrusting cut goes straight to its target instead of ending in mid-air, this same whipping action will take place. The natural whipping action of the thrusting cut makes the blade drop.

An extended extremity, such as a protruding arm, is an excellent target for the vertical cut. The vertical thrusting cut ends with the blade biting down, ripping forward, then snapping up again - all in a continuous action. Keep full thrust's distance from opponent's nearest extremity. If nearest target is hand or forearm, execute a thrusting cut. The blade is cocked in preparation for a wrist action to supplement the natural whip.

The Saw

The **saw** is executed by placing the knife on the subject's body and firmly sawing back and forth. Like the hack, the saw is ideal for use in very close quarters because it can inflict damage to the enemy without great risk of the Practitioner injuring themselves. The Saw is best applied to boney areas of the body.

The Hack

The **hack** is delivered by using the knife to chop with. The hack is used primarily in very close quarters. The Practitioner will rapidly chop with the edge or the spine into boney targets. Like the Saw, the hack is ideal for use in very close quarters because it can inflict damage to the enemy without great risk of the Practitioner injuring themselves. The hack is best applied to boney areas of the body.

The Moulinette

A **moulinette** can be performed when a Practitioner extends their blade in attack and wish to make a second attack without retracting their blade. The Practitioner can perform a vertical or horizontal cut from the wrist as a follow up attack.

The Pommel Strike

The **pommel strike** is executed by striking with the bottom of the knife in a hammering motion.

Six Basic Pommel Strikes

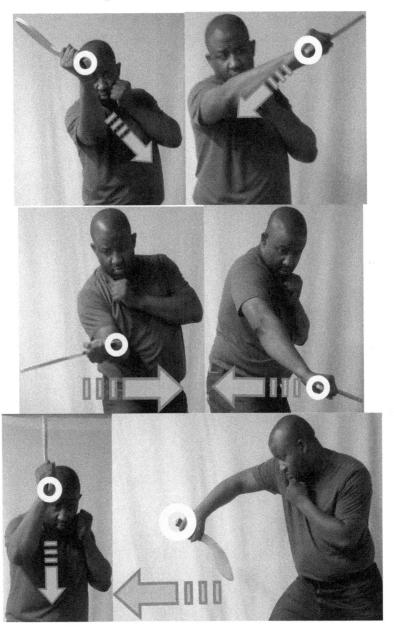

SAFETY IN TRAINING

SAFETY IN TRAINING

Safety must be the paramount consideration during any training activity. We train so that we can protect ourselves and not get hurt. Why then would we allow being hurt in training? It is the responsibility of the instructor and all class participants to ensure the safety of all. All participants in a training activity should be led through a proper warm up and stretching routine before class begins.

Safety Equipment

You should also use appropriate safety equipment for all training sessions. Equipment that should be used includes:

- Athletic Cup
- Forearm shields
- Athletic Mouth Piece
- Safety Goggles
- Safety head gear
- Safety Gloves

Safety Training Weapons

You should also use safe training weapons. A variety of training blades, bludgeons and pistols should be used from rubber to aluminum trainers. NO LIVE WEAPONS SHOULD EVER BE ALLOWED IN THE TRAINING AREA. A good friend of mine was working in a seminar with another instructor. The Instructor drew his blade and cut my friend across the inside of his forearm as part of his demo. The only problem is that he drew his *live* blade and not a trainer. Luckily, a few stitches were all that were needed that day. I shudder to think what would have happened if the instructor would have been demonstrating a *neck* cut?

Whether you reading this as a novice or an experienced pactitioner, it is advisable to train with training we apons that simulate an actual Kukri knife, but that are at the same time incapable of accidentally drawing blood.

The same holds true when you are training with a partner and when you are training solo. Every knife instructor that I know has been accidentally cut despite his expertise, so my counsel here is not based on any assumptions of you being inexperienced, unskilled, or inept. It's based on the knowledge that accidental injuries from small knives are never fun and potential injuries from large knives can ruin your day, if not worse.

Listed below are suitable Kukri trainers that popular with Kukri aficionados. They are constructed of rubber, high-impact plastic, and aluminum, respectively. There are others, as well, and some time spent researching may reveal different models that may be more to your liking. I would, however, caution against dulling, blunting, or taping up an actual Kukri knife simply because you want to "get used to its heft and movement." Not only is that a waste of a good knife, or of a cheap knife, but a dulled, blunted, and taped Kukri can still hurt you if you drop it on your foot or swing it too close to your body. Choose and use a Kukri trainer from among those which are already manufactured for your training safety!

Cold Steel *Kukri Trainer*

Each trainer has been carefully fashioned to look as realistic as possible so they can be effectively used in solo practice, training drills, disarm drills, and demonstrations and any other activity where you want a reasonably close approximation of realism but not the extreme danger and risk associated with an actual knife.

- Material: Santoprene
- Practice safely
- Carefully fashioned to look as realistic as possible
- Blade length: 8 inch
- Overall length: 17 1/4 inch

Keenedge *Kukri II*

Made from auminum, with paracord-wrapped handle in choice of colors.
Overall Length: 16"
Blade Length: 10"
Blade Width at widest point: 2"
Blade width at narrowest point: 1-3/16"

Tak Knife *Gurkha Kukri*

The Kukri is well known as one of the most powerful chopping blades ever invented; practice with our trainer to reduce the chance of injuries with a live version.

This Kukri trainer measures 17" overall, with a 10-3/8" edge, and a thick palm swell.

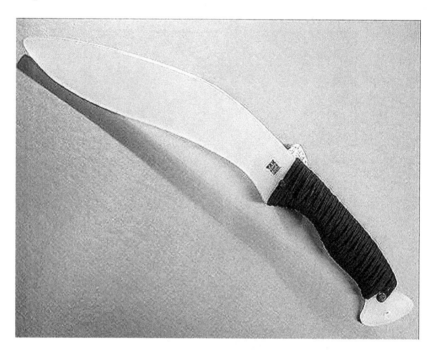

Other Training Considerations

- Training should be conducted in reasonable proximity of emergency medical care

- Training should be conducted in a designated training area with adequate flooring, padding and ventilation.

ADDENDA

ADDENDA

This section contains addenda that are pertinent to the Gurkhas and the Kukri but not directly related to the preceding chapters. The information provides the reader with additional perspectives on this unique knife in the contemporary setting, as well as on the men who still use them.

Addendum A

Murder on the Maurya Express

There are many accounts of the incident involving Bishnu Shrestha, a lone Gurkha who single-handedly routed dacoits and bandits on the Maurya Express. While it's difficult to determine which is actually correct, the account below is the one posted by Shrestha's father. Note: *the English translation we obtained is stilted, but we chose not to change a single word.*

—The authors

Gorkha soldiers have long been known the world over for their valor and these khukuri-wielding warriors winning the British many a battle have become folklore. A retired Indian Gorkha soldier recently revisited those glory days when he thwarted 40 robbers, killing three of them and injuring eight others, with his khukuri during a train journey. He is in line to receive three gallantry awards from the Indian government.

Slave girl Morgiana in the *Arabian Nights* used her cunning to finish off Ali Baba´s 40 thieves, but Bishnu Shrestha of Baidam, did not have time to plot against the 40 train robbers. He, however, made good use of his khukuri to save the chastity of a girl and hundreds of thousands in loot.

Shrestha, who was on the Maurya Express to Gorakhpur from Ranchi while returning home following voluntary retirement from the Indian

123

army, saved the girl who was going to be raped by the robbers in front of her hapless parents, and in doing so won plaudits from everybody.

The band of about 40 robbers, some of whom were travelling as passengers, stopped the train in the Chittaranjan jungles in West Bengal around midnight. Shrestha was in seat no. 47 in coach AC3.

The Maurya Express

"They started snatching jewelry, cell phones, cash, laptops and other belongings from the passengers," Shrestha recalled. The soldier had somehow remained a silent spectator amidst the melee, but not for long. He had had enough when the robbers stripped an 18-year-old girl sitting next to him and tried to rape her right in front of her parents. He then took out his khukuri and took on the robbers.

"The girl cried for help, saying, *You are a soldier, please save a sister*," Shrestha recalled. "I prevented her from being raped, thinking of her as my own sister," he added. He took one of the robbers under control and then started to attack the others. He said the rest of the robbers fled after he killed three of them with his khukuri and injured eight others.

During the scuffle he received serious blade injury to his left hand while the girl also had a minor cut on her neck. "They had carried out their robbery with swords, blades and pistols. The pistols may have been fake as they didn´t open fire," he surmised.

The train resumed its journey after some 20 minutes and a horde of media persons and police were present when it reached Chittaranja station. Police arrested the eight injured dacoits and recovered around 400,000 Indian rupees in cash, 40 gold necklaces, 200 cell phones, 40 laptops and other items that the fleeing robbers dropped in the train.

Police escorted Shrestha to the Railways Hospital after the rescued girl told them about his heroic deed. Mainstream Indian media carried the story. The parents of the girl, who was going for her MBBS studies, also announced a cash award of Indian rupees 300,000 for him but he has not met them since.

"Even the veins and arteries in my left hand were slit but the injury has now healed after two months of neurological treatment at the Command Hospital in Kolkata," he said showing the scar. "Fighting the enemy in battle is my duty as a soldier; taking on the dacoits in the train was my duty as a human being," said the Indian army nayak, who has been given two guards during his month-long holidays in Nepal.

"I am proud to be able to prove that a Gorkha soldier with a khukuri is really a handful. I would have been a meek spectator had I not carried that khukuri," he said.

Shrestha (right) **receiving awards for gallantry**

He still finds it hard to believe that he took on 40 armed robbers alone. "They may have feared that more of my army friends were traveling with me and fled after fighting me for around 20 minutes," he explained.

Addendum B

Prince Harry Made Honorary Gurkha

In October of 2008, Britain's Prince Harry was graced by being made an Honorary Gurkha by fearsome warriors he served with in Afghanistan. An article in the British *Daily Mail* news reported that the renowned Gurkha soldiers paid the royal officer the ultimate tribute by presenting him with a Kukri—their dreaded combat knife— as a token of their esteem. The Gurkhas have a reputation as fearsome warriors who wield the infamous Kukri in battle.

Prince Harry with the Gurkhas in Afghanistan

Lance Corporal Bhim Garbuja of the 1st Battalion Royal Gurkha Rifles (RGR) had served in Helmand Province under Prince Harry earlier that year and described him as a favorite among the troops. The Nepalese soldier said, "We felt he deserved it. He is a good officer and we worked well under his command."

Harry, who was 24 at the time and an officer in Household Cavalry Regiment, went to Helmand Province in December 2007 to work as a Forward Air Controller, serving at Garmsir in southern Helmand and Musa Qaleh. But his four-month deployment was cut short after ten weeks, when a news blackout broke down at the end of February.

Captain Surya Gurung from the 1st Battalion summed up the importance of the gift to the young royal.

> "We don't normally give it as a present to people. Those who we give it to have earned it themselves. It's not necessarily presented to him because he is a Prince; it was because he was so liked by the soldiers. He contributed to the camp and raised the morale of the boys. Hereafter he should consider himself a Gurkha Officer because he was there in that particular time of operations *on the frontline*. That really mattered.

Addendum C

Gurkha Ignores Knife Wound To Trap His Mugger

While anyone with any knowledge of military history knows better than to mess with a Gurkha, but the knife-wielding mugger in this drama was clearly not a military historian. Instead, he pushed Taitex Phlamachha, a former member of the famous fighting force, up against a wall and demanded money. In the fight that ensued, a knife blade was buried in Mr Phlamachha's arm—but he still managed to get the better of his attacker.

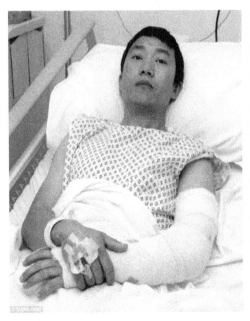

The 38-year-old Phlamachha, a shop owner, was taking an evening walk with his wife Asha when they stopped to look in the window of a health shop in Maidstone, Kent. That's when he was suddenly he was hurled against a wall and allegedly told to "hand over the money or be stabbed."

The former soldier and black belt in karate and taekwondo warned his attacker: "Don't mess with Gurkhas. We're trained to fight." The pair fell to the ground where the mugger knelt on Phlamachha's chest and tried to stab him.Phlamachha blocked the attacks and at the same time even managed to throw his mobile phone to his wife so she could dial 999[1].

Later, the heroic ex-soldier explained he tried to warn his assailant. "I told him, *You need to know who I am*. But he didn't listen. My wife was terrified he was going to kill me. She was screaming for help so I threw her my mobile phone. Eventually I threw him off me but he tried to push my wife over. I kicked and punched him, then I heard him say, *I'm in trouble now*. Then I saw the knife handle on the floor with no blade and noticed all the blood coming out of my arm. I thought, *I'm in trouble too*."

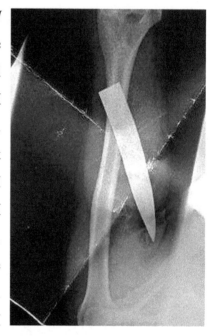

X-ray of blade in arm

He then disabled him with a kick before holding on to his clothes with one arm to stop him escaping for a full 15 minutes. The Iraq and Afghanistan veteran had no idea he had a blade in his arm until he saw the knife handle on the road. "I was holding onto his hoodie but

---

1   The emergency number in Britain.

he took it off, so I just held on to his T-shirt instead until the police arrived."

They rushed him to Maidstone Hospital where an X-ray revealed there was a six-inch blade left stuck in Phlamachha's arm. He was then transferred to Tunbridge Wells Hospital, Pembury, where surgeons removed the blade. His attacker, Jamie Hall, 39, of Maidstone, has been charged with attempted robbery, grievous bodily harm with intent, possession of an offensive weapon and common assault. He has been remanded in prison.

Mr Phlamachha, a Gurkha with Maidstone's 36 Engineers for thirteen years before retiring last year to open an off-licence, added: *'I'm proud to be a Gurkha and I'm even prouder to be a father. And I will do anything to protect my family.'*

Kukri Legends, Myths, and Truths

There are, predictably, many myths and tall tales associated with the kukri and Gurkhas in general. One that has persisted for decades is that a kukri must "always taste blood" before it is returned to its scabbard. Another notion, more technically imaginative, is that the cho or kaudi notch in the kukri's blade is used by Gurkhas as an "aiming sight" with which they aim at targets before throwing the blade—and catching it on its return. These, of course, are laughably and completely untrue, but persist as part of the Gurkha mythology nonetheless. The excerpts below are some of the countless other, slightly more reliable, accounts of Gurkhas and their use of the *kukri*.

Kukris, Not Firearms

On coming across a camp of disagreeably-minded Communist Terrorists, who almost always outnumbered us, [the Gurkhas] *tended to drop their perfectly good firearms, draw their fearsome kukri knives and, screaming war cries, charge into the thick of them. My own preference was to fire from behind the thickest tree I could find, thus giving myself a reasonable chance of survival.*

—A. J. V. Fletcher
Operation Sharp End:
Smashing Terrorism In Malaya 1948-58:

The cho or kaudi notch on the kukri's blade is not used by Gurkhas as an "aiming sight" with which they aim at targets before throwing the blade.

Neither is the kukri a boomerang that returns to the hand after being thrown at the enemy!

The *kaudi* notch is *not* an aiming sight for throwing the Kukri

A Thin Khaki Line

Landing at Brunei airport, [the Gurkhas] double-timed into Bruneitown (Bandar Seri Begawan) and soon came in view of the rioters. Forming a thin khaki line across the lone main street, they unsheathed their kukris and stood facing the howling mob. Looking at that silent row of men, their knives sparkling in the sun, the insurgents had some fast second thoughts and slowly began to disband. The troops smartly about-faced, trotted back to the airfield, and flew home to Kuching. Elapsed time to crush a rebellion—under two hours!

—Sid Latham
Knives and Knifemakers, 1974

The Remarkable Weapon

The Gurkha is worthy of notice, if only for the remarkable weapon which they use in preference to any other. It is called the Kukri and is of a very peculiar shape ... In the hands of an experienced wielder this knife is about as formidable a weapon as can be conceived. Like all really good weapons, its efficiency depends much more upon the skill than the strength of the wielder, and thus it happens that the little Gurkha, a mere boy in point of stature, will cut to pieces a gigantic adversary who does not understand his mode of onset. The Gurkha generally strikes upwards with the kukri, possibly in order to avoid wounding himself should his blow fail, and possibly because an upward cut is just the one that can be least guarded against.

When we were engaged in the many wars in India, the Gurkha proved themselves our most formidable enemies, as since they have proved

134

themselves most invaluable allies. Brave as lions, active as monkeys, and fierce as tigers, the lithe wiry little men came leaping over the ground to the attack, moving so quickly, and keeping so far apart from each other, that musketry was no use against them. When they came near the soldiers, they suddenly crouched to the ground, dived under the bayonets, struck upwards at the men with their kukris, ripping them open with a single blow, and then, after having done all the mischief in their power, darting off as rapidly as they had come. Until our men learned this mode of attack, they were greatly discomfited by their little opponents, who got under their weapons, cutting or slashing with knives as sharp as razors, and often escaping unhurt from the midst of bayonets. They would also dash under the bellies of the officers' horses, rip them open with one blow of the kukri, and aim another at the leg of the officer as he and his horse fell together.

—Reverend Wood
Travels in India and Nepal, 1896

ABOUT THE AUTHORS

FERNAN VARGAS

Mr. Vargas is a lifelong martial artist who currently holds a *Menkyo Kaiden* in Bushi Satori Ryu as well as black belts and instructor rankings in Kuntao, Silat, Kuntaw, Jujutsu and Hapkido. As a certified Law Enforcement Defensive Tactics Instructor, Mr. Vargas has taught defensive tactics to law enforcement officers at the local, state, and federal level, as well as security officers, military personnel and private citizens from around the United States and foreign nations such as Canada, Italy, and Spain. Mr. Vargas has developed programs which have been approved by the Police officer training and Standards Board of several states, and adopted by agencies such as the Pentagon Force protection Agency. Additionally, organizations such as the Fraternal Order of Law Enforcement and the International Academy of Executive Protection Agents have given formal endorsements of the programs developed by Mr. Vargas and Raven Tactical International. Mr. Vargas has been an instructor at the prestigious International Law Enforcement Educators & Trainers Association International Conference (ILEETA). Mr. Vargas currently holds instructor credentials in several defensive tactics and combatives curriculums.

As an author Mr. Vargas has published over 30 books on topics such as *Law Enforcement Defensive Tactics*, *Knife Combatives*, the *Tomahawk*, Native *American Fighting Traditions, Crime Survival,* and more. His writings have also appeared in numerous Industry periodicals.

Fernan Vargas is a current Safety Patrol Leader and Trainer for the Chicago Chapter of the Guardian Angels Safety Patrol where he has worked on several high profile anti-crime campaigns. Mr. Vargas is the founder of the official *Guardian Angels Defensive Tactics System*. A program used to teach Guardian Angels and the public a like. Mr. Vargas and the Guardian Angels have demonstrated the *Guardian Angels Defensive Tactics System* for various television stations including WGN Chicago, Telemundo, ABC Chicago, WCIU Chicago, and NBC Chicago

Mr. Vargas has dedicated a significant portion of his career to the study of edged weapons. He is recognized as an edged weapons subject matter expert,. Mr. Vargas holds instructor rankings in several edged weapons curriculums ranging from Native American knife combatives, Kali, Military knife combatives, and several others. He is the only American to be granted the title of *Soma de Cutel* & Vice Instructor by Grand Master Gilberto Pauciullo and the Instituto per le Tradisioni Marziali Italiane. Mr. Vargas has also been awarded the honorific title of *Master Knife Instructor* by his Sifu

David Siewert. and the designation of *Mater At Arms* by Ernest Emerson and the Order of the Black Shamrock.

Mr. Vargas was named *Trainer of the Year* 2011 by the Alliance of Guardian Angels and has been inducted in several halls of fame for his instruction of Defensive Tactics and Combatives. Mr. Vargas has been inducted into several Martial Arts Halls of Fame and has been awarded the Presidential Service Award and the Shinja Buke Ryu Humanitarian Award for service to the community.

www.TheRavenTribe.com
www.RavenTactical.com
www.RavenTalkPodcast.com
www.MartialBooks.com

JAMES LORIEGA

Maestro James Loriega began his formal training in edged weapons in 1967 when he embarked on his lifelong study of martial arts with the late Shihan Ronald Duncan, the "Father of American Ninjutsu." In the mid-70s, after achieving various instructor-level ranks in Asian systems, Loriega gained his first exposure to the western martial traditions under the tutelage of Maitre Michel Alaux, a former coach to the US Olympic Fencing Team. It was from Maitre Alaux, and his assistant at the time, Ms. Julia Jones, that Loriega learned the rudiments of epee and saber. In September of 1980, Loriega founded the **New York Ninpokai**, a training academy for the traditional arts of ninjutsu. It would be ten years until Loriega was again exposed to western edged weapons.

In July of 1990, while conducting ninjutsu seminars in Spain, Loriega discovered the *Acero Sevillano* (*Sevillian Steel*) knife arts of Andalusia. These arts include the use of the *cuchillo* (knife), *puñal* (stiletto), *tijeras* (Gypsy scissors), *baston de paseo* (walking stick) and *navaja Sevillana* (clasp knife).

His summers for the next five years were spent in Seville, and in August of 1996, he received formal certification as an instructor de *Armas Blancas Sevillanas*. At that time, he was also granted permission to open a recognized branch in New York City known as the **Raven Arts Institute**, where he also teaches the use of the Bowie knife and urban combatives.

In January of 2002, Loriega was recognized as a Master in western arts by the *International Masters-at- Arms Federation* (IMAF), based in Milan, Italy. The IMAF, now dissolved, was an organization of professional teachers of Historical and Classical edged weapons. As teachers, their was to disseminate the historical and martial aspects of European fencing and swordsmanship.

*Loriega's extensive writings have appeared in mainstream martial arts publications such as **Black Belt**, **Warriors**, **Inside Kung-Fu**, **Ninja**, and **Tactical Knives**. His first book, **Sevillian Steel: The Traditional Knife-Fighting Arts of Spain**, (1999 Paladin Press) presents an overview of the edged weapons culture, styles, and strategies of this western martial tradition. A second book, **Scourge of the Dark Continent** (Loompanics, 1999), outlines the history and martial applications of the African sjambok (a rodlike whip made* *from rhinoceros hide). His third book is an annotated English-language translation of the 19th century Manual del Baratero.*

Loriega's knowledge and expertise in martial culture has been amply referenced in the works of other authors, including *Ninja: Clan of Death* (Al Weis and Tom Philbin), *Cebuano Eskrima: Beyond the Myth* (Ned Nepangue, MD and Celestino Macachor), and *Shadow Strategies of an American Ninja Master* (Glenn J. Morris.) In recent years, Loriega has been the subject of two broadcast television documentaries produced by Martial Arts View: **In Search of Historical Ninjutsu,** and **Sevillian Steel** (*concerning the Edged Weapon Arts of Spain.*)

Today, Maestro Loriega continues to travel and to train in addition to providing instruction at the **New York Ninpokai** and the **Raven Arts Institute**. Along with Japanese ninjutsu and ninja-related arts, Loriega provides instruction in Mediterranean edged weapons, including the navaja, stiletto, swordcane, and improvised weaponry. When not traveling to conduct seminars, the author divides his time between teaching in New York and training in Seville, Nice, and Milan.

www.TheRavenBlade.Blogspot.com

SUPPLIES AND SUPPLIERS

Sources for Kukri Trainers

Cold Steel Kukri trainer
www.coldsteel.com

Gurkha Kukri trainer
www.takknife.com

Kukri II trainer
www.keenedgeknives.com

Sources for Custom Kukri

www.**TangoZuluBladeWorks**.com

www.**MountainDwarfForge**.com

Printed in the USA
CPSIA information can be obtained
at www.ICGtesting.com
LVHW090539151223
766149LV00047B/37